WHO TOLD YOU
—— THAT YOU WERE ——
NAKED?

Overcoming Anxiety & Depression
by Trusting the Promises of God

DORSEY C. WEST

Copyright © 2025 by Dorsey C. West
All rights reserved.

No portion of this book may be reproduced in any form without written permission from the publisher or author, except as permitted by U.S. copyright law.

This publication is designed to provide accurate and authoritative information in regard to the subject matter covered. It is distributed and sold with the understanding that neither the author nor the publisher is engaged in rendering mental health, medical, religious, legal, investment, accounting or other professional services. While the publisher and author have used their best efforts in preparing this book, they make no representations or warranties with respect to the accuracy or completeness of the contents of this book and specifically disclaim any implied warranties of merchantability or fitness for a particular purpose. No warranty may be created or extended by sales representatives or written sales materials. The advice and strategies contained herein may not be suitable for your situation. You should consult with a professional when appropriate. Neither the publisher nor the author shall be liable for any loss of profit or income, or any other commercial damages, legal damages, medical damages, or physical damages, including but not limited to special, incidental, consequential, personal, or other damages.

First Edition - 2025

To my family.

Thank you for being my greatest blessing on earth.

Table of Contents

Chapter 1: Take Your Power Back & Be Healed 5

Chapter 2: The Foundation: Genesis, Chapter 3.................. 11

Chapter 3: Are You Really Naked?... 18

Chapter 4: Naked Relationships..24

Chapter 5: Naked Finances 32

Chapter 6: Naked Religion... 50

Chapter 7: We Are Not Naked 62

5 Steps to Get Started 66

CHAPTER 1

Take Your Power Back & Be Healed

> "Who told you that you were naked?" the Lord God asked. "Have you eaten from the tree whose fruit I commanded you not to eat?"
> **- Genesis 3:11 (NLT)**

Let me be perfectly clear with you as we begin this journey together. This is a REAL book, for REAL people, facing REAL challenges. And I want you to know that I wrote this book to help myself as much as I wrote it to help you, if not more.

As someone who struggled with serious mental health issues for decades, including chronic depression and anxiety, you can trust me when I tell you that I know how you feel and what you're going through every day.

It's tough and yes, it's a daily battle. When people (especially doctors and therapists) would tell me that I would have to work on overcoming my psychological challenges every day for the rest of my life, I would allow myself to feel completely hopeless and discouraged and basically wanted to just give up on life. The thought of feeling as bad as I did day in and day out until the day I died, had me wanting to do just that because I believed that was the only way that I would ever find lasting relief and finally put an end to my pain.

But I hope you recognized one word that I used above that has been completely life changing for me, and I believe that it can have the same effect on you, too.

That word is: ALLOWED.

We have the power to *allow* ourselves to only hold on to the thoughts and beliefs that we choose to - and it really doesn't take a lot of effort.

If you're anything like me, you've spent so much precious energy trying to resist negative thoughts whenever they pop into your head. It's a never-ending battle that can leave you feeling exhausted and frustrated, which can easily send you spiraling downward into anxiety and depression. Does this sound familiar to you?

I was trapped in this cycle for most of my life, until I learned a completely different approach. Instead of trying to resist negative thoughts, just let them pass. They may have a momentary effect on you, but if you don't try to fight or analyze them, those unpleasant feelings will quickly fade away like when you walk by an open freezer in the grocery store. Just keep moving and within seconds, you won't even think about it anymore. This becomes even easier to do when you don't label your thoughts as either negative or positive and understand what they really are: simply electrical impulses in your brain. Think about this, if you didn't consider a thought to be negative, would you still feel a need to resist it? Or could you just let it go?

Labeling thoughts is a form of judgment. In order to judge anything, we have to compare it to something, a standard if you will, to determine whether the thing that we are judging is good or bad, negative or positive, or right or wrong. Once we stop judging our thoughts, we free ourselves from so much internal pressure and a heavy mental burden is immediately lifted. I truly believe that's why Christ taught so many lessons on the dangers of judgment during His ministry on earth. He was giving us the keys to our freedom – mentally, physically, and spiritually. Many of us judge ourselves (including our thoughts) more than anyone else. That's why we feel so liberated when we stop judging because it typically has a much deeper, personal impact on our lives.

Now, we all know that there are a lot of things that aren't good for us, and we must be able to effectively identify people, objects, and behaviors that we need to avoid for our own safety and well-being. But those decisions should be based on facts (I'm not going to touch a hot stove because it can burn me), versus opinions (a hot stove is *bad* because it can burn me, so I'm not going to use it). See the difference?

So, please use common sense, but don't get caught in the tangled web of judgment because the more you struggle in it, the more trapped you become.

As I mentioned earlier, judgment requires a standard to compare something against to determine whether it's good or bad. These standards are like measuring sticks. They can be based on governmental laws, religious rules, or even family traditions. Any civilized society needs some form of standards or there would be chaos. The problem is, most of us choose to live by standards that we have never taken the time to determine if they are beneficial for us or not.

I once read that our greatest power lies in our ability to define and establish our own standards. In other words, when we can determine and decide for ourselves what is truly good or bad for us, we can reclaim the authority to live the way that we choose to. I can't think of anything more empowering than that, can you?

"Who Told You That You Were Naked?" is about just that – challenging the standards that we live by to put us on the path to true and lasting mental, physical, and spiritual freedom.

God posed this simple, but powerful question to Adam in the very first book of the Bible. I believe that this was by design because it revealed to human beings the secret to overcoming the pressures of this world from the beginning of time.

I'm going to attempt to show you how questioning the standards that you're living by and establishing new, healthier standards in your life can help you overcome mental health challenges like depression and anxiety once and for all, while blessing you with the peace that surpasses all human understanding that I believe is God's gift and desire for all of His children.

I pray that this new way of looking at your life will heal and empower you as much as it has for me, and even more.

I believe that our Creator has infinite names which span cultures, civilizations, and languages since the existence of the first human beings on earth. I have used the name, "God" when referring to our Creator throughout this book because English is my first language and this name is very simple and easily recognized. In the same way, I also use the masculine English language pronouns, "He," "Him" & "His" along with the name, "God" for simplicity's sake and nothing more. However, I want you to feel free to use any name for our Creator that resonates with you as you read this book, and don't let the world convince you that there is one single name, spelling or pronunciation that is "right" or superior to another. God knows our hearts and what truly matters is that we acknowledge, honor, respect, and submit ourselves to Him in our thoughts and actions, no matter what name or pronouns we choose to use.

CHAPTER 2

The Foundation: Genesis, Chapter 3

I believe that God speaks to each and every one of us directly and indirectly in infinite ways. Sometimes God speaks to us in an audible voice, sometimes through our innermost thoughts or intuition, and sometimes through the written word, including the Holy Bible and other sacred texts. Again, the possibilities are endless. So, whenever you "know that you know" that you received a word, insight or instruction from God, I want you to believe it, trust it, walk in it, and be obedient to it no matter what anyone else might say or think. We each have a very personal and intimate relationship with God that is ours and ours alone, and any revelation that you receive is just as valid and important as anyone else's. Never forget that.

The message that I'm sharing in this book is inspired by the Word of God that is given to us through the Holy Bible in the book of Genesis, Chapter 3. I encourage you to stop right now and read this text for yourself, so that you'll have a clearer understanding and context as I summarize it and share the personal insight that God has blessed me with here.

Before we go any further, I want to make it completely clear that I don't take all the events and stories written in the Bible literally or as historical facts. I believe that many of these accounts are allegorical, which means that they are fictional stories used to simplify and explain deeper truths and spiritual lessons that will help us on our individual and collective life journeys. So, in the creation story of Genesis, it doesn't matter if Adam & Eve were two individual human beings or if they are supposed to represent the earliest group of humans on earth. The truth underlying the invaluable life lessons that we can learn from this and other biblical stories is what is important. Too often we get caught up in debating details and miss the message entirely.

When we arrive at the third chapter of the book of Genesis, God has completed the creation of the world, including the first man and woman, Adam & Eve. In verse 1, we are introduced to the serpent, who has Eve questioning what she knows that God told her to be true (and for her own good), which is NOT to eat from the Tree of the Knowledge of Good and Evil. I believe that the serpent represents the negative influences of this world, which are any ideas that contradict the instructions that God gives us daily through the written and spoken word, as well as through our thoughts and intuition. Here, Eve represents the innate wisdom that God has blessed each one of us with.

In verse 5, the serpent (negative worldly influences) continues to tempt Eve (our wisdom) to disobey God's instruction (the Word) and eat the forbidden fruit by telling her that she will gain something that she doesn't have, which is to be like God by knowing what is good and what is evil. If Eve had remembered or even realized that God had already provided her and Adam with everything that they needed to live in perfect paradise forever, there is no way that she could have been tempted by the idea of needing anything more than that. Remember this idea because this is the key to a lifetime of peace and freedom from the negativity of this world and everything that comes with it.

In verse 6, Eve saw that the fruit looked good. In our daily lives, we are constantly tempted by what we see that looks good, whether it's on a screen or in person. So, the world is still playing on our same weaknesses today that it has been since the first human beings inhabited the earth. Same game, different era. Now, how many times have you seen something (or someone) that looked good to you, ignored your better judgment to possess it, and ultimately suffered (and may still be suffering) negative consequences for it? Was it worth it?

In verse 7, after Adam & Eve disobeyed God (and ignored their inner wisdom) by eating from the Tree of the Knowledge of Good and Evil, they realized that they were naked. I believe that being "naked" represents a feeling or sense of lack or need – physical, mental, or spiritual. In a weak and ineffective human attempt to cover their nakedness, they made some primitive coverings by sewing fig leaves together. In my interpretation, the author of Genesis used fig leaves intentionally, because this was one of the least durable materials that Adam & Eve could have used to make clothing from, and it shows how inferior our abilities and resources are to take care of ourselves in comparison to what God provides for us. We will see this point made even clearer later in the biblical text.

In verse 8, Adam & Eve unsuccessfully attempted to hide themselves from the sight and presence of God (which is impossible) because they were ashamed of how they now perceived themselves to be (naked) as a direct result of their disobedience and ignoring the divine wisdom that God had already given them.

In verse 11, God asked Adam, "Who told you that you were naked?" This question is so significant because it confirms that an outside influence or voice told Adam that he and Eve were lacking something even though God, their creator, had already provided them with everything they needed to live their best life possible. Can you relate to this in your own life?

Also in verse 11, God would walk and talk (fellowship) with Adam personally every day. This was a very intimate relationship that God also wants to have with each one of us now. But, when Adam perceived himself as being naked because of his disobedience, he believed that he was no longer worthy of having this personal relationship with God, and so he tried to hide himself. That's what we often do and that's also why believing that we are naked in the sight of God is so dangerous. We deny ourselves of some of the greatest blessings that we can receive when we turn away from God in guilt and shame.

In verses 12 & 13, Adam & Eve play the "blame game" instead of holding themselves accountable and taking responsibility for their own actions. Adam blames Eve for tempting him and even has the audacity to blame God for giving her to him as his mate. Eve blames the serpent (negative worldly influences) for tempting her, but the truth is that she ate the forbidden fruit because she thought that she would gain something more and better than what she had, even though

The Foundation: Genesis, Chapter 3

God had already given her and Adam everything they needed for eternity.

In verses 14 & 15, God cursed the serpent because of what its negative influence did to his beloved children, as any loving parent would. God also established division between humans and the serpent (the world) because it tried to separate His children from Him by telling them (us) that they needed more than what He was providing to them, which was EVERYTHING, including a life in eternal paradise.

In verses 16 – 19, God punished Adam & Eve for their actions. We must understand that everything we do produces either positive or negative consequences and there is no escaping this universal spiritual law.

Finally in verse 21, God showed His unconditional and never ending grace, mercy, and love for His children, which includes you and me today, by clothing them with animal skins. These were far more useful and effective for protecting them and covering their nakedness than some flimsy fig leaves. Being from Chicago, I can tell you without a doubt that I'd much rather be clothed in leather and fur than in fig leaves to protect me from the harsh elements of the world. Wouldn't you want the same thing for yourself? Well, God is trying to provide you with even more than that right now.

God met their needs in a way that was far superior to anything that they could have imagined and done for themselves, even after they disobeyed Him and suffered the consequences for it. Now, they were no longer naked because God clothed them, and they once again had everything they needed. The same holds true for us today. We are NOT naked, and we have everything that we need because God has already given it to us. Don't let the world tell you otherwise because that is what I believe is the root cause of many of our mental health challenges. Keep reading and I'll explain what I mean in more detail.

CHAPTER 3

Are You Really Naked?

"How in the world did I get here?"

That's the question I asked myself as I stared in the mirror minutes after being escorted to my room at a residential mental health facility to treat chronic depression, anxiety, and suicidal ideations.

In the context of Genesis 3, the answer could be found in the question.

Believing the WORLD is what got me there.

But denying the world would get and keep me out.

In my interpretation of the third chapter of the book of Genesis, I said that the serpent, who tempted Adam & Eve to disobey God by convincing them that they needed something more than they were being provided with, represented the world or negative worldly influences.

The world can be any voice or message that is not in line with the will of God.

And how do you know when the voice you're hearing is not the voice of God?

When that voice is telling you to disobey what you know God is telling you to do (or not do) in order to have something (or someone) in your life that you think you need. Or to put it simply, when it's telling you that you are naked and you need to cover yourself by acting against God's will for you.

The sources of these deceptive worldly voices can include, but are not limited to:

- Various media outlets (television, radio, websites, social media, streaming services)
- Family members
- Friends & neighbors
- Coworkers

- Classmates

One of the most impactful lessons that I remember learning in elementary school was the difference between needs and wants. I recall the teacher asking the class to share what we thought some of our needs were. But, after writing them on the chalkboard for a deeper analysis, I realized that most of those perceived needs were just selfish wants.

I fully recognize that as human beings, we have material needs, as well as spiritual needs. If that weren't the case, God would not have provided food for Adam & Eve to eat, a home for them to live in, and clothing for them to wear when they were banished to live in the world outside of the Garden of Eden.

Spiritually speaking, all we need is the love of God, and that's something that that we already have according to several scriptures in the Holy Bible. In 2 Corinthians 12:9 (NIV), the Apostle Paul shares that God told him, "My grace is sufficient for you, for my power is made perfect in weakness." So, as far as God is concerned, we are never spiritually "naked."

Materially speaking, if we're truly being honest with ourselves, all we really NEED is adequate food, clothing, housing, and access to healthcare. Notice that I used the word, "adequate" because almost everything else falls into the "wants" category. So, the question is not whether we need material things, but exactly what are those things and how much is enough? The answer to these questions can mean the difference between depression & happiness, anxiety & peace, insanity & sanity, and ultimately life & death for all of us.

I would venture to say that most people reading this book have more than they need to not only survive but live a relatively comfortable life. In other words, you are NOT naked – spiritually or materially.

The problem is that we let the world convince us that what we have is simply not enough and we'll never be able to get enough, no matter how hard we try to satisfy our perceived needs. This false belief, which isn't based on any valid proof, creates an unhealthy sense of fear and lack within us. These negative self-perceptions drive us to desperately seek out those items and relationships that we think we need to survive and cause us to act in ways that are not only selfish, but can be extremely dangerous and harmful to ourselves, our environment, and each other.

When we choose to play this unwinnable game, it's just like gambling at a casino where "the house always wins." Except in this case, the WORLD always wins.

Let me explain what I mean.

If you do succeed in acquiring everything that the world has convinced you that you need, you're still going to be trapped in an endless cycle of working and spending almost all of your precious resources – including time, energy, and money – on maintaining this lifestyle. And if you don't feel like you're able to get everything you need because you don't have enough resources, you may very well end up spending even more on healthcare and medication to find some relief (both mental and physical), which you'll ironically be looking for the world to provide you with.

So, when the world tells us that we are naked in some way and we believe it, the world ultimately wins because we essentially sell our souls for something that will never fully satisfy us. This is what I believe is the root of most mental illnesses and unhealthy addictions.

But the good news is that there is a way out. And that is simply believing and knowing that we are not naked because we choose to trust that God has already given us access to everything that we need in this life and the next.

That means you are not naked, you never were, and you never will be!

I'm going to spend the remaining chapters of this book analyzing three specific areas of our lives where we tend to believe that we're naked and prove to you that's not the case through honest and sincere self-reflection. Some of these ideas may seem very simple and others may feel a lot more complex, but we need to understand that we are not naked in any area of our lives to feel completely free and at peace. And that is the key to taking control of our mental health and living the spiritually and materially abundant lives that God wants every one of His children to enjoy.

As Christ said in John 10:10 (NLT), "The thief's purpose is to steal and kill and destroy. My purpose is to give them a rich and satisfying life." I believe the "thief" in this scripture represents the negative influences of the world, and that's what we must overcome if we want to be healed.

CHAPTER 4

Naked Relationships

Let's take a closer look at our relationships because that's the area that I believe has the greatest impact on our lives.

This diagram illustrates my personal relationship hierarchy to help you better understand the concepts that I'm going to present in this chapter:

GOD
Family: Spouse, Children, Parents, Siblings, Extended
Friends
Neighbors, Classmates & Coworkers
Acquaintances & Strangers (People we don't really know yet)

Again, this is a general framework for the purpose of my analysis here. Yours may be somewhat different and that's perfectly fine because your life journey is personal to you. However, I truly believe that despite any differences we may have, God must always be placed at the top of any relationship hierarchy because it is the most important one in our lives.

I can tell you from personal experience that if your relationship with God isn't good, then you're not good.

And what defines a "good" relationship with God? If you ask a thousand people, you'll get at least a thousand varying answers because our relationships with God are all very personal. That means it's strictly between you and God whether your relationship is good or not. It's something that you can genuinely feel in your heart and no one outside of you, especially the world, can tell you where you stand with God.

But I can tell you this – wherever you believe that you are in your relationship with God, please know that He loves you and wants to be as close to you as you will allow Him to be in your heart. There are several scriptures in the Bible that demonstrate the depth of God's loves for us. Based on my personal interpretation, the core principles of the Bible are:

1. God loves us more than we can ever comprehend.

2. God has demonstrated His love for us since before the creation of the world.

3. God will continue to love us for eternity.

Once we begin to truly understand that God loves us unconditionally, then our relationship with Him will grow stronger. The Bible tells us in Romans 8:38-39 that nothing can separate us from the love of God. Knowing this is the foundation of a peaceful life because we typically try to turn away and hide ourselves from God when we allow the world to convince us that we have done something so wrong that God doesn't love us the same way anymore and we feel guilty, ashamed, and naked in His sight. That's exactly why Adam & Eve tried to cover themselves with makeshift fig leaf clothing and hide from God after they disobeyed Him and ate from the Tree of the Knowledge of Good and Evil.

The absolute worst thing that we can do when we know that we're doing something that God doesn't want us to do is to *try* to turn away from Him. I'm intentionally using the word "try" here because it's impossible for anyone to distance themselves from God. He is everywhere at all times, so we can never outrun His reach. In fact, we need to do the complete opposite and run into His open arms as fast as we can while admitting the mistakes we've made and take solace in the truth that He has already forgiven us because He will always love us.

You don't have to use any special words or language when you talk to God about your missteps and ask for His help and forgiveness. Just let your thoughts and words flow from your heart because God is all-knowing, which means He already understands how you feel and what you're trying to say. That's how you develop a better relationship with God. Remember that He is telling us throughout the Bible, "You're good with Me. I love you. Come home."

Now here's some more great news…

If your relationship with God is good, all of your other relationships are so much easier to maintain. We know that every human relationship is going to be difficult at some point, but it's how you look at and handle these challenges that makes your relationships feel far less stressful and much more fulfilling. That's because when you know that you're good with God and He loves you unconditionally:

- No one can withhold genuine love from you.

- No one can hurt you beyond healing.

- No one can leave you unprotected.

- No one can take anything away from you that you truly need.

- No one can manipulate you with guilt.

Take some time here to reflect on your most toxic relationships, past and present (but don't get stuck), and I'm sure that you'll be able to relate to at least one of the statements above.

I have been divorced three times (yes, you read that correctly) and I can tell you that every time I entered into one of these marriages, I was holding on to two false beliefs in my heart:

1. I wasn't living up to God's standards for me at that time and I needed to do better in order to regain His love and favor, which in this case was to marry the person that I was in a relationship with.

2. My future spouse had something that I needed to be truly happy and pleasing in God's sight, and they could either give it to me or take it away at any time – with or without warning.

Both of these negative beliefs were based on fear, but now I understand that the only thing that we should fear in life is the power of God. That's because only God has the power to:

- Love you perfectly and unconditionally.
- Heal every wound, emotionally or physically.
- Protect you from anything.
- Provide you with everything.
- Find you guilty beyond forgiveness.

And the Bible teaches us through multiple scriptures and stories that God will always love, heal, protect, and provide for us, while never hurting or condemning us.

Although there were some very valid reasons why my previous marriages failed and divorce was the most viable option for me; I now understand and accept full responsibility for believing the world when it told me that I was naked mentally, spiritually, and materially, and then attempting to cover myself with unhealthy relationships. Instead, I should have asked for and allowed God to cover me with His eternal love and compassion.

When you believe that you are naked, you will look for covering from just about any source, no matter how inadequate it may be, just like Adam & Eve's fig leaves. In other words, we'll grab the first and most convenient covering that we can find and even sell our dignity and souls for it. That's how desperate we can be to not want to feel naked anymore. But inevitably we realize that the covering we are receiving is not sufficient to meet our perceived needs, we feel unfulfilled, and then we try to find covering in someone or something else. This broken cycle of seeking, finding, and seeking again is promoted by the world in movies, television shows, music, books, and other forms of entertainment for its material gain. Unfortunately, we blindly believe and consume this deceptive content to our detriment.

This doesn't just apply to our romantic relationships, either. We participate in this toxic cycle as parents, children, friends, coworkers, and employees - essentially any relationship where we believe that someone else has something that we need to be happy and fulfilled.

- **Parents** – Often seek a feeling of being loved and needed from their children.

- **Children** – Seek provision, protection, approval, acceptance, and love from their parents.

- **Friends** – Seek love, loyalty, and support from each other.

- **Co-workers** – Seek loyalty, recognition, cooperation, respect & support from their colleagues.

- **Employees** – Seek provision, appreciation, and respect from their employers.

So again, when we know that we already have a good relationship with God as our birthright, then we also understand that no human being can give or take away from us anything that we truly need to live our best lives possible.

Don't just take my word for it, either. There are so many places in the Bible that will confirm this for you.

You never have to feel naked in a relationship again. God will clothe you better than any covering you can find for yourself, just like he did for Adam & Eve, especially when you are seeking that covering in human relationships.

CHAPTER 5

Naked Finances

After relationships, the area of my life that has had the greatest impact on my mental health has been my finances. Based on personal observation within my own family and social circles, during my domestic and international travels, and through the messages that the world's media constantly feeds us, I believe that money is a major cause of perceived happiness and stress for most people around the globe.

Notice that I used the word, "perceived" when stating that money can lead to happiness or stress. That was intentional because I'm sure that we have all heard stories or personally know of financially wealthy people who remain anxious and miserable even though they possess seemingly large sums of money. At the same time, there are people living in relative poverty who remain in a state of joy and peace despite their financial circumstances. This just shows that you can still believe you are naked no matter how materially rich you are.

I witnessed this firsthand when I spent a month at a residential mental health treatment center. The facility was very upscale (as mental hospitals go), and there was no way that I could have afforded to be a patient there if I hadn't been blessed with health insurance coverage through my employer at the time, along with the financial support of my family.

In an environment like that, living in close quarters 24/7 and participating in the most intense and transparent group and personal mental health therapy that I've ever experienced in my life, you get to know people very closely from all walks of life. We would often talk about how this level of intimacy would never have been possible under any other circumstances. There were patients there who arrived by private jet and others who took the bus in. Millionaires were living, learning, and healing side by side with working class people like me, but socioeconomic status really didn't matter there. We were all just trying to get better and support one another as much as we could.

There were two treatment tracks or options offered to patients there: mental health and substance abuse. I quickly learned that one of the first questions that patients would ask each other when first meeting was, "Are you mental health or substance abuse?" referring to your assigned treatment track.

The first few days, I was very quick (and even proud) to answer that I was there for mental health treatment and not substance abuse because I didn't want to be perceived as an "addict." But the more I surrendered my ridiculous ego, I realized that we were all addicted to unhealthy thoughts and methods of finding some kind of temporary relief to our feelings of depression, anxiety or other manifestations of mental illness. It didn't matter if it was alcohol, narcotics, pornography, food, self-harm, rage, or any other negative coping behaviors that you can possibly think of, we were all trying to survive a mental health crisis. Participating in multiple group therapy sessions every day helped me to understand that our mental health challenges were basically the same, no matter how we got there or how we were trying to deal with them.

So, what does all of this have to do with overcoming the false feeling of being financially naked?

It doesn't matter how much money you have access to, if you believe that you don't have enough or won't be able to acquire enough to meet your material needs, then you are in danger of feeling so depressed or anxious (or both) that it can cause you to suffer from severe mental illness. This is exactly what happened to me, although I was earning a six-figure income at the time. I can't point to a specific financial setback that caused me to finally break down from all the self-imposed pressure, and it didn't happen overnight. The feeling of being financially naked had been developing in my mind since I was a child because that's when the world started bombarding me with false ideas about material wealth that I accepted as truth because I didn't know any better.

That's how we commonly develop our belief systems. We start readily accepting the information that we receive from the world (our environment) until we make an intentional decision to question those beliefs and determine if they are beneficial for us or not. If they aren't, we need to seek out new information and adopt healthier beliefs. Nothing changes if nothing changes, and the only way to transform our lives is to modify our thoughts, including how we think about money.

I fully acknowledge that money is necessary to survive in our society. There is no getting around that. I can't think of one institution that can be successfully maintained without adequate financial resources, including the church. But the universal question that we all need to consider when it comes to money is this, "How much do we really need?"

I know that I quoted from the Bible earlier in 2 Corinthians 12:9 where it declares that God's grace is sufficient for us. But try convincing a bank to accept grace as payment for your mortgage or auto loan and let me know how that works out for you. You need money to pay bills, plain and simple. Now this doesn't mean that God's grace is somehow insufficient for you because it most certainly is enough. We just need to realize that God gives us grace in unlimited ways, which can and does include material wealth. We need real provisions to live in the real world. Our problem is that we believe what the world tells us we supposedly need, and then we feel naked if we don't have it.

Let me share this story with you to help illustrate my point. I have several items of clothing in my closet that I have accumulated over the years, but most of them never get worn (I'm sure you can probably relate). Yet when I see a new shirt or shoes in a store display, I may still think to myself, "I could use a new shirt" or "I need those shoes." Now based on what I just told you about having so many clothes in my closet that I haven't worn for years, a very valid argument could be made that not only should I not buy anything else to wear, but I should probably be giving most of my wardrobe away.

But, let me continue with my story. One morning, I went into my closet to pick out something to wear to church and I noticed a few tiny black ants crawling on a shirt that was hanging up. This was very strange to me because I would expect to find ants where there was a source of food, like the kitchen, but definitely not in a closet. As I looked closer, I realized that there were more ants crawling on several items of clothing that were hanging on the rack.

Now my focus was on trying to find out where these ants were coming from. As I frantically pushed hangers to one side to get a better view, I could see a trail of little black ants coming from an adjacent column of shelves where I was storing more clothes. As I pulled stacks of folded garments off the shelves, I was shocked and disgusted to find even more ants crawling all over my t-shirts, shorts, hoodies, and sweaters. I ran to the garage to grab some extra-large yard waste bags and filled two of them with my ant infested wardrobe. The idea was that I was going to take all of my precious clothing to the local laundromat and use their big commercial machines to wash the ants away and reclaim my stuff. After placing the bags outside I determined that at least 60% of the clothes that I owned had been affected and needed to be washed before I could wear them again.

The bags of clothes sat outside most of the day and by the time I got back home, I didn't feel like spending hours at the laundromat. So, I told myself that I'd wash them the next day. Well, fast forward almost a year later and those same bags of clothes have been sitting in my garage, still unwashed and unworn since the day I discovered those ants.

So, what is the point of this story? My wardrobe was unexpectedly reduced by over half of the clothes that I owned, and I haven't even missed them. Life went on and having fewer items of clothing to wear has not prevented me from doing anything that I wanted to do. That just confirms that I've been spending too much money on things that I never needed in the first place for years. I wonder if I would have felt as financially naked as I did at times if I had some of that money in my pocket instead of hanging in my closet, serving no apparent purpose?

Clothes shopping has and continues to keep so many of us in debt, especially when we use credit cards to make those purchases. But based on the personal experience that I just shared, we don't really need most of the clothing that we buy. And the same concept applies to many of the other items that we spend our money on including food, housing, vehicles, electronics, and more.

It all goes back to my elementary school lesson about needs versus wants. Just because we see something that we like or want doesn't mean that we need it. Especially considering that our likes and wants can change quickly. So, if we spend a lot, if not most, of our money on things that we don't really need, how would our lives look and feel if we simply stopped doing it?

The world tells us that we need more money to buy more things that we don't truly need because the world stands to gain from it. Marketing is basically someone telling us that we need something and they are the ones who can fulfill that need, but at a cost. It is estimated that the average person can be exposed to anywhere from 4,000 to 10,000 marketing messages each day, depending on lifestyle factors such as screen time, location, and the types of media that we tend to consume. Now that most of us carry smartphones during virtually every waking hour, the world has even more access to our eyes and ears and uses these opportunities to constantly communicate to us that we are naked in some way. We even start our days by waking up to inboxes full of messages telling us what we need and how we can quickly and easily fulfill those needs for an unbelievably low price, with just a few taps on the screen.

We all have a finite amount of money to spend, no matter what our income sources are. When the cost of our perceived needs exceeds the amount of money that we have access to, whether it's cash or credit, our feelings of stress, anxiety, and depression can and often do increase as a result. I know from experience the mental anguish that can come from not being able to pay your bills. But, instead of viewing the solution as acquiring more money, what would happen if we made the decision not to accumulate unnecessary debts in the first place? It's a much simpler and easier path to peace, but it will require us to ignore what the world tells us that we need and believe that we are not naked because God can, does, and will provide us with all the material and financial covering that we require.

I can almost guarantee that if you take an inventory of all your material possessions, you will realize that you can reduce them by half and still maintain your current quality of life. Now I'm not suggesting that you go out and indiscriminately give away everything you own or join the minimalist movement. I'm just asking you to genuinely consider what your life would look like with approximately 50% less of the things you currently own and make an honest determination of whether your life would be better, worse or remain basically the same. I think you'll be pleasantly surprised by what you discover from this exercise.

I am certain that if I realized that I didn't really need most of the money or possessions that I believed I did to live a truly abundant life, I wouldn't have found myself in that mental health treatment facility. At that time, I was so discouraged because I had convinced myself that I would never earn enough money to retire or enjoy a lifestyle that was on par with my "successful" peers (primarily based on what I was seeing on social media) that I allowed feelings of anxiety and depression to literally push me to my breaking point. I was even struggling with suicidal ideations because I felt like I had wasted my life and all of my opportunities to become financially prosperous. To put it simply, I believed that I was naked according to the world's standards and there was no way for me to ever adequately cover myself, even though I was blessed with an income that put me close to the top 10% of earners worldwide. In one sense, I was correct – I never would be able to acquire enough based on what the world determined that I needed. But what I didn't understand yet was that God could cover my family and me in far superior ways to anything that I could ever get from the world. I just needed to remember and trust His promises.

It's not that we don't need food, shelter, clothing, housing, and an income to pay for it all. The fact is we don't need nearly as much as the world has convinced us that we do, and an honest look at our lives will show us that God is already providing us with everything that we truly need. But we need to assess what we have by God's standards and not the world's standards because according to the world, we will never have enough, and believing that can lead you down the path to insanity. I know it because I lived it, and I don't want you to experience that if I can help it. Making an intentional effort to live by the simple philosophy, "If I don't need it, I won't buy it," can save our lives and give us lasting peace of mind.

Throughout this chapter, I've been using clothing to illustrate my point that unnecessary spending is the primary reason why many of us feel financially naked because it's arguably the easiest material item for us to accumulate in excess. I recently learned that clothing waste, caused by the millions of tons of apparel that we throw away every year globally, is one of the greatest sources of environmental pollution in the world today. In countries like Ghana, in Africa, discarded clothing from other nations is literally washing up on their shores every day and causing major health problems for their citizens. This crisis provides us with some of the most compelling evidence that proves we are not naked (literally and figuratively) and that we already have way more than we will ever need. It is both saddening and mind boggling to think that there are people in the world who don't have adequate clothing to meet their basic needs while many of us throw away perfectly wearable clothing because we just don't want it anymore. Yet we worry about not having enough money to the point that it can negatively impact our mental health.

I'd like to focus now on what are typically our two greatest expenses: housing and vehicles. Do we need a safe place to live and reliable transportation? Absolutely. Do we need to spend as much money as we do on these things, to the point where we can potentially make ourselves mentally ill when trying to figure out a way to pay for them? Absolutely NOT.

How do we find ourselves in positions where we are stressing about how to hold on to houses and cars that we can't comfortably afford? I believe it's because many of us measure success, wealth, and even God's blessings by the quantity and cost of our material possessions. In other words, the more stuff that you accumulate and the more you pay for it, the more proof you have that you're wealthy and successful. Otherwise, you wouldn't own all these things, right? But having something and being able to afford it are two totally different things, and understanding this is the key to feeling covered financially instead of feeling naked.

The world wants us to believe that our worth is determined by our possessions so that it can keep us enslaved in an endless cycle of spending and debt, which it continues to profit from. When we can't keep up with this cycle, it fuels our stress, which can manifest in anxiety, depression, and other forms of mental illness. But guess what? The world will even profit from this by selling us pharmaceuticals and treatments for the mental illnesses that we succumbed to by participating in its never-ending spending game.

Again, I am not suggesting or encouraging you to sell your house and cars. Everyone has different needs, and safe housing and reliable transportation are essential to maintain a relatively good quality of life for most of us. However, if holding on to where you live and what you drive is stressful to you because of the limits of your financial resources, then you need to stop right now and make an honest assessment of whether you should continue to live in **that** place and drive **that** vehicle. Downsizing can literally be lifesaving.

Trust me, we can all live with less and still be happy. It's funny when I think about how most of my childhood friends and I grew up in what we considered to be very comfortable homes in Chicago that had just one bathroom to share for families of 4, 5, 6 or more. Most of us also didn't live in houses that had central heating and air conditioning systems to deal with the brutally cold winters and extremely hot summers. Yet I don't remember anyone complaining about their living conditions at home. But now, most of my peers would never consider living in a house without at least two bathrooms and a good HVAC system, even if they live alone. The point that I'm trying to make is that we really can survive and even thrive with a lot less if we choose to. But housing and transportation are more of a status symbol for many of us now. We believe that we must show and prove to each other that we are not naked according to the world's standards by where we live and what we drive.

Like housing, vehicles can be one of our greatest sources of debt, along with anxiety and unhappiness, if we can't comfortably afford to own them. Again, the car we drive has become visual proof of how blessed we think we are. How many times have you seen luxury automobiles with personalized license plates that read some variant of the word, "blessed"? But do you recall ever seeing a car tag like that on an older, rusty vehicle that looks like it may have been involved in several accidents? The truth is, if you have reliable transportation then that's yet another way that God has richly blessed you. You just need to recognize and appreciate it. We all do.

Our jobs, which most of us need to earn money and survive in this world, can also drive us down the path of mental illness if we judge our careers and income by the standards that the world sets for us. I remember working in a very stressful office environment and a frustrated friend and colleague came into my office to vent about some things that he wasn't happy with at work. In fact, he was so fed up with our emotionally toxic workplace that he was seriously considering leaving our place of employment for good. When I expressed my concern about how he would pay for his expenses and take care of his family, he said something very profound to me: "I need A job, not THIS job." And he was absolutely right. Within a few weeks, he had moved on to another company, earning even more money and with much less work-related stress. God provided him with even better financial covering, and here was a person who questioned the very existence of God. Yet his material needs were still taken care of, and he never believed that he was naked, either.

On the other hand, I was a professed child of God and follower of Christ, but I was still hesitant to try to find a better career opportunity because I was afraid of being financially naked without my current employer providing a reliable income for me. After weeks of encouragement from my former coworker, I eventually applied for and was offered a much better paying job at his new place of employment, but it would have required me relocate and I didn't want to move my family at that time. But that experience reminded me of God's never-ending grace and allowed my feelings and fear of financial nakedness to start melting away. Within another month, I was recruited to another company for a position that paid more than twice as much as what I was currently earning and I was also able to work from home, which eliminated my commute and the stress that went with it. So, not only did God show me once again that I was NOT naked, but that He can and will provide covering that is far better than anything than we can fashion for ourselves. We must have the faith to believe and do what we know that God is telling us and not what the world is telling us. That is the key to experiencing peace, happiness, healing, and abundance beyond our limited imaginations. To say that understanding this truth has helped me to overcome my strongest mental health challenges is an understatement, and I want the same for you, too.

Again, I fully acknowledge that we need material things to survive and that we need to work to earn a living. And there is absolutely nothing wrong with acquiring or experiencing things that provide you and your family with comfort and joy, including vacations and other luxuries. But we don't need so much of any of these things that it causes us unhappiness and stress, especially to the point that we are experiencing any form of mental illness. It's not worth it and it's certainly not necessary.

Do you still believe that you need more money to cover your financial nakedness? Well, the fastest and easiest way to have more money is to simply spend less of the money that you earn. Maybe you don't need to find a better paying job, but instead you just need to reduce some of your expenses. Will the world, including your family, friends, and colleagues question if you're in some kind of financial bind or consider you to be less successful if you have fewer possessions? Probably, and let's be honest, as human beings we all care about what people think and say about us to some degree. I believe that's what can make scaling back and downsizing so difficult for us. But don't let that stop you because contrary to what the world tries to convince us seemingly every moment of every day, we are not naked. Not because of what we have, but because of who God is to us - our provider.

When we believe God and not the world, we understand that we will always have everything we need and being stressed over what we don't possess is our choice. I choose to be at peace now and you can, too. No matter how financially naked you feel and how much debt you may currently have, take comfort in knowing that you always have a way out and it starts with letting go of things that you don't really need. It's just that easy.

And let me tell you that the most amazing life transformation begins when you stop trying to cover yourself and allow God to cover you by following His guidance. Just as with Adam & Eve, our inferior "fig leaves" can never compare to God's superior "animal skins." His covering can be provided to you in infinite ways including food, clothing, housing, transportation, employment, and so much more. Quiet your mind, open your eyes & ears, and be willing to receive the opportunities that God will lead you to. Remember, less is often more, and your blessings may come by releasing things that you own instead of increasing them. Remember, your peace is worth more than any of your possessions.

When you start living by these principles, you will be able to see more clearly what you truly need and don't need. You'll easily recognize the things that lift you up and those that are dragging you down. When you have the faith and courage to tell the world, "No more!" you will realize a feeling of genuine peace, healing, and restoration that you have never experienced before. And it's a feeling that you will never want to let go of, either.

Trusting God's promises to provide me with everything I need, along with being a very active participant in specialized therapy from qualified, trusted professionals (who God will also lead you to when you seek them out) is how I am able to overcome lifelong mental health challenges, including chronic depression and anxiety. This transformation did not happen overnight, and it's still something that I have to work on every day. But I can tell you with certainty that your life can and will improve drastically if you trust God and put in the work that it takes to get better, because that is His promise to us. We are not naked, we never were, and we never have to be.

CHAPTER 6

Naked Religion

As I reflect on my decades long struggle to overcome anxiety and depression, I realize that my religious beliefs contributed to my mental illness just as much as my feelings of being naked in my relationships and finances, if not more.

I can honestly say that I have never had any issues with God, whatsoever. God has never let me down and always provides me with more than I could ever need. I'm good with God and always have been.

But religion is an entirely different story. I have had major internal conflicts with religious rules, philosophies, rituals, and especially expectations for most of my life. The root of this conflict and confusion was between what I felt in my heart and what most well-meaning people taught me about what my relationship with God was supposed to look and feel like.

I was raised as a Christian, and for most of my life my understanding was that a man named Jesus was also God, and although He loved me so much that He died to pay for all of the bad things that I've done (and would do), He would still punish me severely if I did any number of things to displease Him – whether I was aware of them or not. These offenses included even THINKING about something that I shouldn't, which was especially difficult for me because my mind races constantly. I felt like I had relatively good control of my actions, but my thoughts often ran wild (and I still have to work at this every day). Knowing that kept me in a constant state of fear that I was going to unintentionally think of something that was offensive to Jesus, which would then draw the wrath of God, and I definitely didn't want that.

Here is the cycle that I was trapped in:

1. The world tells me that I am naked in some way, and I believe it.

2. I use whatever limited resources I have at my disposal to cover this perceived nakedness.

3. I experience increasing levels of anxiety because my covering doesn't feel adequate.

4. I feel hopeless because I believe that I will never be able to fully cover my nakedness, and that leads me into a state of depression.

5. I feel guilty because I believe that I must have done something to offend God, and He caused me to be naked as a consequence of my actions.

6. I remain in a state of fear that God is going to continue to punish me by taking or withholding someone or something from me that I believe I need to cover my nakedness.

7. I pray desperately for God to forgive me and help me to become a better person so that I won't think or do anything else to displease Him.

This became the framework of my thinking ever since I first "ate" from the Tree of the Knowledge of Good and Evil, which in my case was when I began to learn about Christian doctrine as a child.

It wasn't until I was almost 50 years old that I was formally diagnosed with Attention Deficit Hyperactivity Disorder (ADHD) and Obsessive Compulsive Disorder (OCD), which only made these cycles more frequent and intense while I remained untreated. I am now happy to share that after years of praying for relief and finally receiving the specialized therapy that I needed to effectively treat OCD, I no longer meet the criteria for a clinical diagnosis, and that has helped me to break this exhausting cycle. From a spiritual perspective, this demonstrated to me that prayer does work, but it takes dedicated action to make it effective.

So, let's talk about prayer.

Prayer is a word and a concept that is central to many religions because it is universally recognized as our means as human beings to communicate directly with our creator. In my Christian upbringing, I came to understand that prayer basically worked like this:

Close your eyes, bow your head, and preferably get on your knees to appear as humble as possible before God. Then, using a reverent tone (verbally or in silent thought), proper grammar, and your most advanced vocabulary, ask God for what you want (or don't want). Making deals with God like, "If you give me this, I'll stop doing that," was a common practice. Finally, include some requests for others to show that you aren't selfish and increase your chances of getting your prayers answered. The more you prayed showed how much you believed in God, and the more blessings you would receive.

That is how I determined that prayer worked based on years of Sunday School lessons, sermons, classroom instruction (when I attended Lutheran schools), and personal observations of other Christians.

As you can imagine, it took a huge mental toll on me, especially when I believed that certain prayers were not being answered even though I believed that I was doing it the "right" way. That surely meant that I was being punished for being a sinner, even if I didn't understand what I was doing that was so wrong.

Thankfully, I have a different and simpler perspective on prayer now (even though old, ingrained beliefs die hard). I now believe that prayer is a two-step process: ask & act. Doing one without the other isn't nearly as effective as doing both steps together.

Let me give you an illustration to help explain what I mean.

Imagine if you bump into me on the street and you ask me how I'm doing because I don't look so well. I then explain to you that I haven't eaten a meal in two days because I'm having some financial difficulties and I just can't afford to buy any groceries right now.

Now here is an opportunity for both of us to use prayer to help meet my immediate need of finding something to eat and my overall need to cover my financial nakedness.

I can ASK God to provide me with groceries to make some meals to satisfy my hunger, as well as an opportunity to earn money to meet my financial needs. Then I can ACT by offering to complete any jobs or tasks that you would be willing to pay me for so that I can generate some income to buy inexpensive staples such as beans, rice, potatoes, and pasta to feed myself for multiple days.

You can also ASK God to provide me with food to eat and an immediate source of income. Then you can ACT in several possible ways: let me borrow a few dollars to purchase some basic groceries, buy the groceries yourself, purchase a meal for me to eat, or allow me to do some work for you to earn the money that I need to buy food.

Action is a requirement for effective prayer according to the teachings of Christ in the Holy Bible. Jesus instructs us in Matthew 7:7 (NIV), "Ask and it will be given to you; seek and you will find; knock and the door will be opened to you."

As you can see, after telling us to ASK for what we need or want, Christ commands us to SEEK and KNOCK, which are both actions.

It doesn't always take a lot of action, but it will take at least some action to see results.

PRAYER = ASK + ACT

Now what if we revisited the same scenario above, but this time we both just bow our heads, ask God to provide me with a meal to eat, and then go our separate ways? How much less effective would that be in meeting my needs than if we also took some of the actions that I suggested?

Telling someone that you'll pray for them sounds good and may even make both parties immediately feel better, but "nothing happens if nothing happens," and I believe that we must put effort behind our words if we sincerely want God to answer our prayers and cover our spiritual and material nakedness.

Again, if we ask God to bless us with a new job, but we never take the action of applying for one, can we really claim that God didn't answer our prayer if we don't get another position?

I believe that religion can be a very useful tool in strengthening our connection to God, but the ultimate goal is for each of us to have a deep, personal relationship with Him. Remember, when you know that you're good with God, the world can't deceive you into believing that you are naked and that you need its limited material resources to cover you at the cost of your peace and mental health.

So, please work every day on building an intimate connection with God through simple prayer (ask + act) and let Him guide you to recognize and accept the spiritual and material covering that He wants to provide you with because it is custom made just for you. That's far better than the inferior, overpriced, off-the-rack coverings that the world can ever offer you.

I appreciate the guidance and framework for life that the Christian religion offers me, but I value my personal relationship with God even more because whenever I get confused or unsure about any aspect of my religious doctrine, I know that I can go directly to the source and get clarity.

The last thing that I'll share about feeling naked in religion deals with the challenges, struggles, and hardships in life that we all must deal with sometimes, no matter how "good" we think we are.

One of the worst periods of depression that I can remember going through was during the six months or so after I graduated from college. Receiving my bachelor's degree was my greatest achievement at that point in my life. I was the valedictorian and was asked to accept the Presidential Charge for my graduating class, which meant that I had an opportunity to speak in front of my classmates, family, and friends. The president of the university even hugged me onstage afterwards to the ovation of the audience. I felt like I was on top of the world and nothing could stop me from accomplishing anything that I wanted to.

But upon returning home to Chicago, those feelings of invincibility quickly faded, and I found myself living in my mother's house with no plan, no direction, and struggling to find a job, let alone a fulfilling career. I really didn't know what I wanted to do, anyway. The assumption was that I was going to attend law school. But, I realized that was the "safe" response that I gave everyone when they asked me what I was going to do after college because it sounded good, and no one ever questioned me about it.

I soon found myself almost completely out of the money that I had received as graduation gifts, staying up watching television until 4 AM, and waking up around noon or even later some days. I had battled depression before, but nothing like this. I felt like I had fallen from the highest to the lowest point in my life in a matter of weeks, and I was totally unprepared for the tremendous toll that it took on my mind and spirit.

At that time, I wasn't comfortable with any religious doctrine, although I desperately tried to find one that resonated with me. I loved and trusted God, but I believed that you had to subscribe to a particular religion in order to have a good relationship with Him, so I felt completely naked in that sense. When I would share some of my personal struggles with my family and friends (who were primarily Christian), I felt more blame than empathy for my situation. They would tell me that the reason why I felt hopeless, directionless, and depressed was because I wasn't "in the church." The message that I was receiving from people who meant well and genuinely cared about me was that if I would wholeheartedly accept the same religious doctrine that they subscribed to and actively participated in it, then God would take away my challenges and struggles. In other words, the mental and financial hardships that I was going through were the direct result of my spiritual deficiencies and could be easily remedied by simply going to church and leaning into religion.

Instead of encouraging me, this advice drove me deeper into a state of hopelessness and even resentment because I did not believe that Christianity (or any other religion that I was familiar with) was the right path for me to discover and develop the strong connection to God that I sincerely wanted and had been longing for since I was a child. I wanted to please Jesus and God so that I could have my prayers answered and live a comfortable, pain free life, but I just didn't know how to do it. Again, the world was telling me that I was naked because I hadn't fully embraced Christianity, and I believed it. This made my feelings of anxiety and depression even worse.

I'm not blaming religion or the people in my life who truly loved me and were offering me the same solution that helped them overcome their personal challenges for the way I felt. But now I believe and understand that what the Holy Bible teaches us, especially through the ministry of Christ, is that God wants to have a close, personal relationship with each one of us, just as he walked and talked with Adam every day in the Garden of Eden.

I also know now that we will all face personal challenges and hardships. That is an inescapable fact of life on this earth. When we do inevitably encounter those struggles, it is NOT because God doesn't love us or that we are somehow disconnected from Him because we don't subscribe to a specific religious doctrine. In fact, failure in life is a requirement for success. I can tell you from personal experience that when we stop believing that we are naked according to the world and we start trusting God to cover us spiritually and materially, the hardships that once seemed impossible to overcome will feel a whole lot easier to manage and move past. Yes, we will still feel mental and physical pain, depending on what we're going through at the time, but we can find peace and comfort in knowing that we will overcome it because God will always cover us – even if we don't go to church. But trust me, a strong church home and family will help you more than you can imagine. And this is coming from someone who never felt comfortable in a church setting for most of my life.

Understanding and accepting God's promises to always provide for us has had a tremendous, positive impact on my mental health and I know that it can have the same effect on your mind and spirit, too. Just never forget that when it comes to you and God: Relationship > Religion. And as Romans 8:38 reminds us, NOTHING can separate us from His love.

CHAPTER 7

We Are Not Naked

I want to thank you for taking this journey with me. My hope and prayer is that at the very least, God has allowed me to help you see your life in an entirely new light by understanding that He loves you and that you are not naked, no matter what the world tries to tell you.

But please don't just take my word for it. Go back and read Genesis, Chapter 3 with this new perspective and ask God to give you more clarity and understanding as you do.

You should also read different stories and scriptures in the Bible for even more confirmation of God's love and promises to provide us with everything that we need and more.

Finally, practice keeping your eyes, ears, and heart open to see, hear, and understand God speaking to you and guiding you to His eternal spiritual covering, and away from the temporary covering that the world is trying to offer you. Remember what Christ teaches us in Matthew 6:33 (NLT), "Seek the Kingdom of God above all else, and live righteously, and He will give you everything you need."

If you are struggling to overcome any mental health issues, please know that victory is not only possible, but promised, when we trust God, pray, and persevere. It is crucial to your healing process that you work with a mental health professional that you trust and feel comfortable with. It won't be an easy process, and it will take a lot of time, energy, and continuous hard work, but the relief that you'll eventually start to feel will make it all worth it and motivate you to keep going. You must understand that maintaining your mental health is something that you have to work on every day to achieve lasting results. You may also have to meet and work with several counselors, therapists, psychologists, and psychiatrists before finding the right one for you at the right time in your life. For me, it took years before I assembled my "dream team" of mental health professionals, but please stay encouraged and trust God's guidance because receiving and actively participating in the treatment that you need can give you the happy, peaceful, and abundant life that you may have never believed was possible for you.

The world's objective has always been to deceive you into believing that you are naked in some area of your life, whether it's relationships, finances, spirituality, material possessions, and the list goes on and on. We are bombarded with messages (especially commercial marketing) from so many different sources that tell us we don't have something that we really need and only the world can offer it to us. But remember that the price of your mental health and peace of mind, not to mention the majority of your financial resources are not worth anything that the world can provide you, and it will never be enough. There will always be something more that you will be tempted to believe that you need, but you really don't and never did in the first place.

God's grace is sufficient (remember 2 Corinthians 12:9) and His provision is plenty. We just need to remember the difference between needs and wants and not fall into the trap of trying to possess everything that we think we want because the world tells us that this is how we are supposed to show each other that we are successful and blessed.

We can absolutely enjoy so many things and experiences beyond what need to survive, but we must also be able to recognize when having those things is a source of stress and leading us down a path that can potentially end in anxiety, depression, hopelessness, and even death. As someone who has been to the brink of complete mental collapse and brought back by the grace of God, I can tell you that anything or anyone that requires you to trade your sanity to get and keep is never worth the cost.

God has covered us since the beginning of our time on earth, and He always will. Take the first step to restore your mental health by making a commitment to trust God to provide you with everything that you need spiritually, mentally, and materially, and boldly tell the world, "No, I don't need that from you because I'm not naked!"

Your life will never be the same. And the peace, joy, and abundance that you've always wanted will be available to you. It always has been, you just didn't realize it because you thought that you were naked in some way.

But now you know:

- I am not naked.
- You are not naked.
- We are not naked.

I love you and may God continue to bless you on your journey to complete healing and restoration!

5 Steps to Get Started

I don't believe that this book would be complete without giving you a concrete plan to start your new life journey. We all need some guidance, and I pray that these steps will provide a good foundation for you to make some positive, lasting changes in how you think and live. Please don't feel like you need to do everything exactly as I've laid it out here. Trust the voice of God in your heart and mind, and please try to work with a licensed mental health professional whenever possible.

Before you begin, I strongly encourage you to pray to God for wisdom and guidance to keep leading you on the path that He wants you to take. Remember that acting is the second step of prayer (ask & act), but you don't want to move blindly, and you want every decision you make to line up with God's plan and purpose for your life. And yes, you will stumble, fall, and make unwise choices every day because we are all imperfect humans. But don't let that discourage you and always remember that God's grace is unlimited and sufficient for us. So, keep moving forward and feel yourself getting stronger as you overcome each challenge, no matter how many mistakes you make along the way.

STEP 1 – Recognize Your Riches

Get a pen and some paper (I suggest using a new spiral notebook) and start writing out everything in your life that you are grateful for. It's important that you use pen & paper because in this digital world of screens that we live in, writing things down can make them even more impactful to you. This list should include people such as family and friends, material possessions like clothing, homes, and vehicles, your physical health (even if you're experiencing some issues, appreciate the areas of your body that are functioning well), and anything else that you are grateful for, no matter how big or small.

As you write down the people and things in your life that you're blessed with, you should start feeling more loved and appreciative of what God is providing to you every day, even if you feel like your life isn't going exactly the way you want it to right now. This can also help you realize that you may have been overlooking so many other blessings, which could give you a positive new perspective on your life.

Hold on to this list and revisit it often because it can encourage you to stay motivated and moving forward when life starts to feel overwhelming.

STEP 2 – Secure Professional Support

If you're seriously committed to healing, I believe that it is absolutely necessary for you to find at least one mental health professional that you feel comfortable working with. But let me warn you – finding just the right counselor, therapist, psychologist, or psychiatrist can be a relatively long and sometimes frustrating process. So, be prepared to exercise a lot of patience and perseverance during your search, especially if you start feeling discouraged.

Anytime you experience a mental health emergency, including if you're thinking about harming yourself (or others) in any way whatsoever, please call local **Emergency Services** (**dial 911** from any phone), the **Suicide and Crisis Lifeline** (**dial 988** from any phone), or go to your nearest medical Emergency Room facility **IMMEDIATELY** and try to explain to them as clearly as possible what you're thinking and feeling. This is the time to be completely honest and transparent, so that they can provide you with the assistance and resources that you need. Please let a friend or family member know what you're about to do so they can support you, whether in person or over the phone. Just having someone with you that you trust as you seek help during a crisis can make the situation feel a lot more manageable.

If it's not an immediate emergency (and there is **ZERO** possibility or threat of you harming yourself or anyone else), you can search online for "mental health professionals near me" (or indicate a specific city or zip code). Then, go through the list of results, call the phone numbers given, and explain how you are feeling and that you are seeking a mental health professional to talk to. You may reach an answering service (especially for solo practitioners because they may be seeing a patient at the time you call), so please leave a detailed message and be sure to include your best contact information. If you don't hear back from the people that you left messages for after 24 hours (or the specific follow-up time that they may have indicated on their answering service or website), then please call back. Sometimes mental health professionals handle every aspect of their practice by themselves. So, it's not that your message isn't important to them, they may just be behind on some of their administrative tasks like returning phone calls. Eventually, you'll have the opportunity to talk with potential providers and begin to build the relationships that you need for your healing journey.

STEP 3 – Assemble Your Army

You can't do this alone and thankfully you don't have to. Believe it or not, there are millions of other people trying to heal from and overcome the negative effects of believing that they are naked in this world - mentally, physically, and spiritually. And if they're not, then they probably know someone very close to them who is and want to help in any way they can. That means that there are also potentially millions of people that may be willing to stand with you as you face these challenges. It may begin with just one person, but that can quickly evolve into a huge support network of family, friends, peer groups, mental health professionals, and more. But you must have the courage to share the things you're struggling with (sometimes with complete strangers) and ask for the help that you need. Start today by talking to someone that you trust about this journey to mental healing and recovery that you're about to embark on and ask if they will commit to supporting you by at least checking in regularly and being available to talk via text, voice or both when you need them. Give them the contact information for your mental health professional if you have it, and let your provider know about this support person, as well. Your small team may very well end up growing into a powerful army, but it can start with just one person. Remember, you are NEVER alone, and you never have to be. That's one reason why God put us all on this earth together.

STEP 4 – Clean Your House

Remember the notebook that I recommended you get in the first step? Well, now I want you to pull it out again and this time make a list that contains two columns. Label the columns, "Needs" and "Wants." This list will include all of the things that you spend your resources on, both financially and emotionally (including relationships). As you build your list, think very carefully about what are actual needs and what are really just wants.

Once you have your list written out, review each item in the "Wants" column and think about how you can reduce or eliminate it completely. For items in the "Needs" column, determine how much is truly necessary and how much you can possibly reduce and still live comfortably. For example, if you put groceries in your "Needs" column, think about the specific foods that you can eliminate that aren't good for you. Yes, you need to eat, but do you need to eat *that*? When it comes to material items such as clothing or electronics, determine what you can give away or even sell to earn money for investing in yourself.

Sometimes we become very emotionally attached to certain things, and I know that makes them more difficult to part with. When this happens, I really want you to consider if a specific item is helping you or hurting you. Make another list with these two columns: "Help" & "Hurt" and place those things (including relationships) that you're having a difficult time deciding what to do with in the appropriate column. Remember, this list is all about helping you improve your mental, physical, and financial health, so be completely honest with yourself. In fact, you may even want to make a separate list just for the people or relationships in your life because this is what we typically spend most of our resources on, whether it's time, money or energy.

Take as much time as you need to complete these lists and review them thoroughly. Focus on removing as many things as you can from your "Hurt" column, as soon as possible. It will probably be very difficult in the beginning, but it will become easier the more you do it, and you'll start feeling better about the changes that you're making in your life. As you update and act on these lists regularly, you'll start realizing that you have more time, energy, and money at your disposal than you've ever had before.

STEP 5 – Move With God

I saved the best for last. As I've said several times in this book, if your relationship with God is good, then you're good. Now, I can't tell you exactly how you should connect with God because each individual relationship with Him is very personal and unique. But I can tell you that it starts with listening to the voice within you. Some call it your conscience. Some call it intuition. I call it the Holy Spirit, and it can communicate with us in infinite ways. You may see or hear something while walking down the street, and it has such a deep and personal meaning that it feels like you are receiving a special message just for you. I believe that is God speaking to you through the Holy Spirit. You can even feel it when you're doing something that you know you shouldn't do, so try to listen and obey because it will probably save you a lot of heartache and pain. Of course, we'll all stumble and fall. But stand up and get back on your path as soon as you can, remembering that God loves you and forgives you.

I believe that Christ died on the cross as a perfect sacrifice for our sins, and because of that, we will enter the Kingdom of Heaven when we leave this earth if we just accept that truth. Try to find other followers of Christ, whether it's a small group or a big church, and study the scriptures of the Holy Bible together – especially the Gospel. I know that there are so many denominations, sects, and schools of thought that it can be confusing. But this is why you need to focus on quieting your mind for a least a few minutes every day and listening for the Holy Spirit to guide you to the people and resources that you need at the right time, from mental health professionals to other brothers and sisters in Christ.

Please accept the fact that you are going to face many obstacles and setbacks, but each one also provides you with an opportunity to grow when you overcome them. So, look at these challenges as blessings and gifts from God, rather than punishment. Stay the course, stay encouraged, and stay faithful. Remember that God has promised to always love, protect, and cover us, and He never fails!

BONUS STEP – Connect with Community

I'm building a community online at **www.WeAreNotNaked.com**. It is constantly evolving, as we all are, but our mission is to provide safe spaces to share, learn, and support each other as we not only overcome our mental health challenges, but the world itself. We hope to see you there sometimes and look forward to the positive energy that we know you'll bring. Remember, you are NEVER alone and there are more people out here that want to help you than you realize. Visit us online anytime, introduce yourself, and let's grow together.

May God continue to bless you, keep you, and cover you!

Scan the QR code to connect with our online community.

www.WeAreNotNaked.com

www.ingramcontent.com/pod-product-compliance
Lightning Source LLC
Chambersburg PA
CBHW060422050426
42449CB00009B/2089